Sketches
of Hales Owen II

by Bill Hazlehurst

A second album of forty pen & ink sketches
of local buildings, some new, some old,
and some just memories.

****
Quercus
John Roberts
8 Hillside Close, Bartley Green
Birmingham B32 4LT
****

Sketches of Hales Owen II

by Bill Hazlehurst

ISBN 1 898136 12 2

First Published 1996

Dedication

To my wife Margaret, for all her help and support.

Contents

HALES OWEN
simplified map.

Refer to list of
Contents for names.

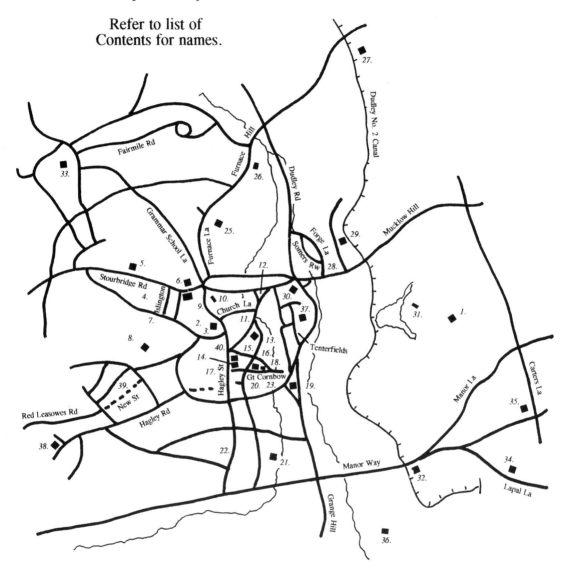

The Artist

Bill Hazlehurst was born in Smith Street, Hockley, Birmingham in 1936, where his father was a policeman at Kenyon Street Police Station in the Jewellery Quarter and his mother a glass and silver worker. At Summer Lane Secondary School he had a good art teacher, a Miss Savage. His last school years involved two days a week at Vittoria Street Art School in the Jewellery Quarter learning silversmithing. Apart from this he is a self taught artist.

Starting work as a metal engraver, he switched at 19 to repairing mechanical accounting machines. Over the next thirty years he saw them replaced by electric models, then in turn, electronic valve, transistor and microchip machines. All the time Bill was retraining, and he was also sketching portraits of fellow engineers and machine operators.

Laurel and Hardy changed Bill's life in 1987 when, acting in a skit for charity he fell and smashed his ankle. Bored with idle time in hospital and at home in Hales Owen, Bill turned to his sketching. No human models were available, but an interest in the history of Hales Owen had turned up some old photos of the town. In this period Bill changed his technique from pencil to pen and ink.

Voluntary redundancy followed Bill's spell off work and he was able to develop his paying hobby into a business. Now he has a shop at Hagley Road, Hasbury, Hales Owen where he sells his own pictures and the work of other artists. Bill is married with two married daughters with two grandsons and a grand daughter.

Photo: Glynnis Bateman

Hales Owen

Bill's first album of Hales Owen sketches came out in the Autumn of 1993, and in it we gave a short history of the town. Not every reader of this book will have the other, so we have prepared a new version which gives much the same basic facts.

Hales Owen lies on the south-western edge of the West Midlands area which stretches nearly twenty miles to the north, and slightly more from east side to west. It is a busy place, with the main routes from the south to Dudley running through, and the main road to the west nearby. Even so, Hales Owen has a small, market town atmosphere which is quiet, settled and pleasant. The town has also been on the edge of history, with no local battles, revolutions, sieges or plots. Local people think the redevelopments of the 1950's and 60's were severe changes, but it is still a place which holds much of its essential character. Hales Owen has evolved without drama but has its own well loved buildings, corners and streets, and has made its modest contribution to events.

The Manor of Halas is first mentioned in William the Conqueror's Domesday survey. A manor of course, referred to an area of land rather than a house. This one had the usual list of hides, carucates, bordars, cottars and radmen, whatever they were, which were all worth 25 shillings a year. The land was held by Sir Roger de Montgomery, Earl of Shrewsbury, since his contribution at the Battle of Hastings.

After the Conquest land was owned by the Crown, and holdings were granted to powerful tenants for services, or various reasons of expediency. Their heirs would inherit the title, so land could remain in the same family for generations. Later it might be forfeited and return to the Crown, for example, if the holder rebelled against the King or his family ran out of heirs. The land might then be awarded to a new tenant or remain Crown property for a while. Hales Owen has reverted to the Crown several times, once for as long as 75 years.

St John's Parish Church was started by Roger de Montgomery in 1082 to replace a small Saxon building. The round arches in the nave and the west doorway are Norman, but there are some Saxon remains in the west side.

In 1102 Robert Belleme, third heir of Roger de Montgomery, lead a rebellion against Henry I and the estate was forfeited to the Crown. There it remained until 1177, when Henry II gave it to his Welsh brother in law, Dafydd ap Owain. There is no doubt that *owen* or *owayn* had been added to the name Halas by about 1205. A court roll, or record, dated 1270 refers to *Hales Owayn*.

Originally then, the name was in two words, which later became Hales Owen. The question remains whether that is still the name, because they can change over the centuries. No one has called Quinton "Cwenington" or Rubery "Rowberrie" for centuries, much as we might prefer them, but use of Hales Owen is much more recent. Local opinion seems to be that the single word title first appeared on road and railway signs, and not through popular usage. People can remember signs reading *HalesOwen* in the 1950s, and you can find it still on the board of St Margaret's Church, Hasbury. Bill has for years been conducting a low key campaign for the two word version, and a lot of people seem to like it, so that is what we shall use.

On Dafydd's death the Manor again reverted to the Crown, until King John granted it to the Bishop of Winchester in 1214 to build a monastery. Bishop Peter was entitled to establish whatever order he chose and the Abbey was built by the Premonstratensian Canons, named after the area of Picardy where they were founded in 1120. Goodness knows how they introduced themselves, but because of their vestments local people most likely called them the White Canons.

The Abbot obtained a Charter granting Borough status from Henry III in 1272, and you can see a copy of the document in Birmingham Reference Library. Hales Owen already had regular fairs and markets; being a Borough enabled it to have more, and therefore increase its wealth. Coal mining in the district is first mentioned in 1281 and again in 1307. The town is on the southern tip of the famous Ten Yard Seam, the biggest coal seam in the country, which runs north through the Black Country, Wednesfield, Cannock and under Cannock Chase.

Possibly because of local apathy, the Borough Charter was allowed to lapse. However Borough status was granted again in 1936 by Edward VIII, allowing us to have a Mayor and Alderman once more. This book coincides with the 60th aniversary of the event.

In 1498 Hales Owen had a visit from Prince Arthur (age 12), eldest son of Henry VII. This would hardly be worth mentioning except (sniff) to point out that it was the last Royal visit until 1957.

Hales Owen Abbey was dissolved in 1538 with all other monasteries. Most of the contents and fittings went to the parish church, where you can see some of the Abbey floor tiles.

The estate was granted to Sir John Dudley, later Earl of Warwick and Duke of Northumberland. Whilst urging the boy King Edward VI to support the Protestant cause, he quarreled with the Catholic Princess Mary. When the King fell ill and Mary seemed likely to succeed to the throne, Dudley tried to replace her by her cousin, Jane Grey, who was married to one of Dudley's sons. The plan failed, Dudley was executed with Jane Grey and the estate again reverted to the Crown. On later appeal from Dudley's widow Joan, it was regranted to her.

Joan's heir was another Sir John Dudley who sold the manor to Thomas Blount and George Tuckey, who very soon sold it to Sir John Lyttleton His family has been associated with Hales Owen ever since. In 1627 Adam Littleton was born, apparently not a relation of the Lord of the Manor but son of the Vicar. He became a churchman and classical scholar who wrote a Latin dictionary.

In 1652 Hales Owen's Free School was founded. Charitable gifts to the Borough for several purposes were being misused or unused, so the Commissioners had them pooled to fund a school to teach the children of the people of Hales Owen. It became the Grammar School in 1863.

The first reference to industry occurs in the mid 1600s. A gun barrel mill and other iron and slitting mills were working on the River Stour, and nail making developed as a cottage industry from the early 1700s.

William Caslon was born at Cradley in 1692. He was the first great English typefounder and in 1734 issued a specimen sheet of his own founts.

"... though not bred to the art of letter-founding, has, by dint of genius, arrived at an excellency in it unknown hitherto in England, and which even surpasses anything of the kind done in Holland or elsewhere."

and this is a sample of Caslon Bold

William Shenstone was born in 1714 and his grave is in St John's church. He was a mediocre poet but a noted landscape gardner who laid out the gardens of his home, The Leasowes. They attracted visitors from fashionable society and entranced even the deeply religious and austere John Wesley:

" ... I was never so surprised. I have seen nothing in all England to compare with it. It is beautiful and elegant all over. There is nothing grand, nothing costly; no temples, so called; no statues, (except two or three which had better have been spared) but such walks. such shades, such hills and dales, such lawns, such artless cascades, such waving woods, with waters intermixed, as exceed all imagination! ... "

In 1783 Thomas Attwood was born, a political reformer who supported the Reform Act of 1832. He was the first MP for Birmingham and a Chartist leader. The Dudley No.2 Canal was cut in 1792 from Netherton through Hales Owen to join the Worcester & Birmingham Canal.

Records of some of these people and events can be found in the sketches, such as the Abbey Infirmary and the Parish Church. But many pictures are of buildings erected since 1800. Hales Owen developed with the rest of the West Midlands in this period, making anchors, tubing, lenses, horn buttons, ornaments and fertilizer, wirework, firebricks, stainless steel, drop forgings, presswork and the famous toffee.

Bill has drawn the schools, pubs and houses, streets and shops, cinemas, foundries and factories and churches - all part of the life of the area. Some still stand, many can only be remembered; but through all his pictures runs a feeling of things evolving slowly in a quiet and settled place, aside from the great dramas of history.

The Sketches

The pictures are mixed into no particular scheme although some connected views are in sequence. You will probably find many places difficult to recognise because some of the buildings no longer exist and the views are from different periods. Bill's drawings come from whatever sources are available, including photos of varying quality taken at any time over more than a hundred years, supplemented by research and his own recollections and observations.

Neither this book nor the first album attempt to offer a complete history of Hales Owen nor an architectural analysis of the buildings. The notes on each picture are brief and personal. However, there are comprehensive and authoritative books on the town's past from which you can learn much more.

1. The Leasowes

This grand old brick house was probably built on the slopes of Mucklow Hill in the 17th century, and here William Shenstone was born on 18th November 1714. The house was bought by his grandfather who moved from a farm at Illey. He left a son, Joseph, to continue there, while the other son Thomas and his father raised livestock at The Leasowes.

Thomas Shenstone married Anne, eldest daughter of William Penn of Harborough Hall near Blakedown. Thomas died in 1724 and his father (William's grandfather) in 1726. Anne then managed the farm until she died. There were two sons, Joseph and William, who came under the Guardianship of Rev Dolman, Rector of Broom - Annes' brother in law.

Joseph was trained as a lawyer, though he never practised, and William became a poet. However, Rev Dolman, died in 1745 so William had to manage The Leasowes estate. Gradually he began to see the west facing slopes of the estate as the picturesque landscape which became so fashionable in the 18th century. He moved and planted trees to create views, built follies including a ruined priory and a hermitage, and put up statues. From a stream he conjured pools and waterfalls which were crossed by little bridges. The Leasowes was known as one of the finest examples of landscape gardening.

William Shenstone died in 1763, but his heir had no creative flair. He impoverished the estate by felling the trees for timber, then sold out. The estate had thirteen owners between 1763 and 1865 and in this period the old house was demolished by a Mr Horne, who built the present house.

The Leasowes. c 1761.

(8)

The North Gate, St. John's, Hales Owen.

(9)

2. Parish Church of St. John the Baptist

St John's stands on the sandstone hill which forms the centre of Hales Owen, so you can see it from many different heights and angles and the 160 foot high steeple is visible from miles away. The first book featured three views, but this is closer, and emphasises that very curious octagonal tower. The north gate is the traditional Bride's entrance.

The earliest part of the present church is Norman, the work of Roger de Montgomery, Earl of Shrewsbury. Nothing remains of an earlier Saxon building. Like all churches, St John's has been much altered and extended over the centuries. This warm and rosy sandstone is lovely to look at, but weathers so badly that it is a cause of anxiety all over the Midlands.

The War Memorial was built around 1922 to honour local men who died in the Great War; the names of victims of World War II have been added.

3. The Old High Cross

What is left of the old cross stands in a corner of
St John's churchyard, having survived several moves,
amputation of its arms, being heaved over in a gale
and a spell on a rubbish tip.

It may originally have come from St Mary's Abbey
and been set up in the church grounds at "Laconstoon Field". In 1469 a law restricting the brewing
of ale says: *"and from Laconstoon by the High
Cross up to the Cornebowe, one brew."* This field
is probably occupied by the Cornbow Shopping
Centre, and appropriately, for the cross marked
the site of the town's market and fair. By a grant
of Henry III, market day was on Wednesday, but
people found this inconvenient and it was changed
to Tuesday by Edward III.

Some time around 1500 the market and the cross were
moved to Cornbow. The arms were removed to comply
with new laws at the time of the Reformation of the
church by Henry VIII, but otherwise it remained at the
Cornbow until 1908, when a great gale threw it down.
The Rural District Council cleared the site and the old
cross was dumped on a tip, but it was rescued by a Mr
Alfred Homfray. Eventually a Mr Job Garrat paid for
erection where it now stands.

The ball finial is said to have been part of the
church's ancient porched gateway, which was demolished about 1790. During demolition of a house in
1915 a cross head was found, and Bill wonders if it
came from the market cross which might have been
hidden at the time of the Reformation.

The Old High Cross, Hales Owen.

Stourbridge Road, Hales Owen

W. Hazlehurst

(13)

4. Stourbridge Road

These two sternly nonconformist Victorian chapels,
Zion and the Baptist chapel, still stand, but are now
commercial premises. The cottages were demolished only a few years ago and the sites are car
parks. Fortunately the new work is not displeasing,
but there is nothing about the scene to make you
quake at the knees about your sins.

5. The British School

Education was made compulsory in 1870 and became
free some twenty years later. Lessons were delivered
in Sunday schools and workshops and managed to give
the children some primitive learning. Demand grew
but the Sunday schools could not cope with their inad-
equate facilities and few teachers. The non-conformist
churches (The British Society) and the Church of
England (The National Society) started to build
their own day schools.

The Baptist Sunday School in Stourbridge Road was
built by Mr W Caleb H Bloomer, a wealthy iron manu-
facturer who lived at Heywood House on Mucklow
Hill. Sunk into the school floor was a large font where
Mr Bloomer's converts were baptised as only a Baptist can. It was rediscovered when the school was
demolished a few years ago.

During the week the building was used as a Ragged
School to give free lessons to poor children until
in 1878 it became The British School. It was taken
over by the County Council in 1908.

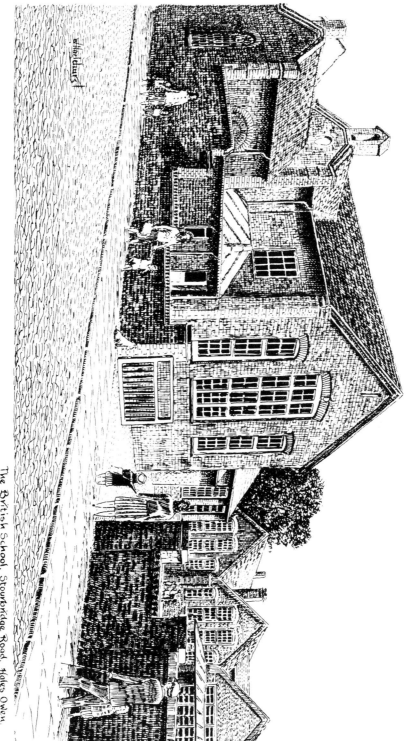

The British School, Stourbridge Road, Hales Owen.

The Picture House, Stourbridge Road.

6. The Picture House

This was one of Mr Bernard Bray's chain of cinemas and was built in the 1930s, a little before the Lyttleton on Hagley Road. The Picture House was in brick and replaced a timber framed affair which had been destroyed by fire. Photographs taken from the church roof show it as painted to resemble a black and white half timbered Tudor house.

The cinema closed in the 1960's and was later demolished. It would have faced the Baptist Chapel on Stourbridge Road from where the Conservative Club now stands.

The Lyttleton Cinema appeared in the first book of sketches where we pointed out that it was quite a nice example of a "between the wars" "Gaudeon" style cinema facade. You can see the same ideas in the Picture House, but it seems far too quiet and restrained.

7. Islington

These rows of early nineteenth century terrace houses formed one of the town's old streets, between Stour-bridge Road and Richmond Street. In common with others in the Black Country and Bromsgrove, many had nail making shops in the back yards.

Nail making in this area was a cottage industry, that is - carried on in the worker's homes, which cont-inued longer than most others. Spinning and weaving for example, had long moved into factories where the owners could benefit from large and efficient mach-ines. Towards the end of the 19th century demand for these nails declined because even the economies of having no large plant and paying pitiful wages could not match those of fast working machines.

Iron wire and orders were put out to the workers by middle men, who sold them on to wholesalers. Many of these later became employers with factories, and two such firms sprang up in this area, Attwoods & Faulkner and Harry Rudge. They started with the bulkier types of iron work for the building trade, such as brackets and hooks.

At various celebrations such as coronations, royal jubilees and the ends of the both World Wars, the people living in these streets would decorate them. Branches cut from trees in the grounds of the Rectory in Richmond Street were nailed to the walls.

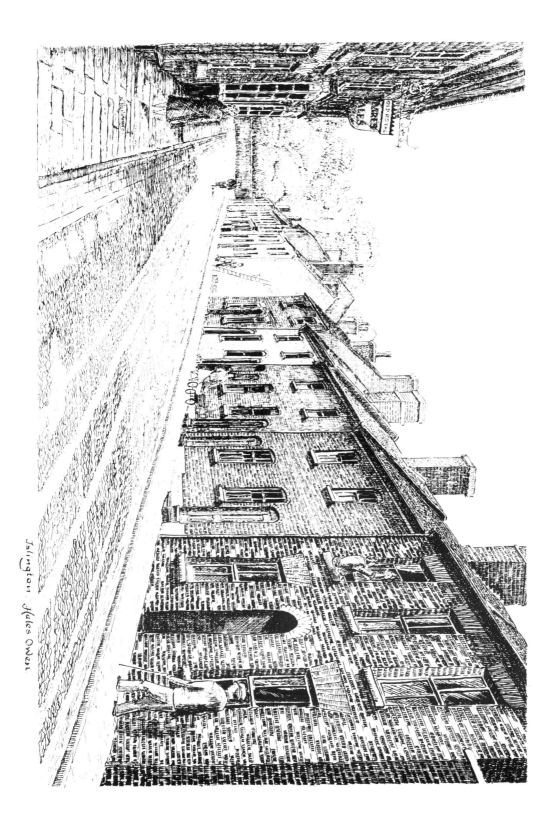

Islington Hales Owen

(20)

Highfield Recreation Grounds, Hales Owen.

8. Highfield Recreation Ground

Flats in Andrew Road were built on the lower slopes of the Recreation ground, but it is still there in much reduced form, and without paddling pool or bandstand.

This view from the west shows St John's church and an idyllic rural landscape on Mucklow Hill. In the top left corner you can just see the MEB office block.

Obscured by tall flats and tall trees and with buildings in the middle ground, this prospect has gone the way of the bandstand. However, if you stand so that you can see past the flats looking to the right of this picture, the distant view is still surprisingly green.

9. Church Street

This view from the church gate can be roughly dated from the cars, with an obvious Moggie Minor - note the early type of registration plate, a (probable) Triumph Spitfire and (possible) Baby Austin.

 In the centre of the picture is the old Conservative Club which was demolished when the big traffic island and pedestrian underpass were built at the Townsend. The Club was rebuilt in Stourbridge Road. The shop on the right was Edge's which sold school uniforms. Perry's on the left sold furnishings. Only the George Inn at the far left still stands.

Church Street, Halen Owen

The Old Workhouse Lock-up, Hales Owen.

(25)

10. The Old Workhouse Lockup

Attempts to date this picture depend on how you place the moustached and plus foured cyclist and his machine. However, its location relates is to the previous picture because the Workhouse, built by Lord Lyttelton, stood in Church Street opposite the George. All workhouses had a lock up to deal with the misdemeanours of the inhabitants.

This one was a small, two storey building in the local red sandstone which was removed to build Midland House and the car park. The bricks were all number-ed as it came down, and it was thought that it might be rebuilt in a suitable place in Hales Owen or at the Avoncroft Museum. However, nothing was done and it now lies at the Abbey as a heap of rubble, brick numbers long gone. Perhaps some day someone will organise rebuilding.

11. Church Lane

This is perhaps the most picturesque view of Hales Owen and has been drawn by many artists. No set of local pictures is complete without it. We included similar one in the first book of sketches, but this showed the cottages on the left more frontally and excluded the pub.

The timber framed building contained four houses which may well have been built in the late 14th century. Being so close to the church, their earliest use might not have been domestic. The roof of one cottage caught fire in the 1950s but they have all survived their five centuries intact. Recently renovated, the group is now one of the jewels of Hales Owen.

The Malt Shovel was once a big pub which turned the corner at the top and continued along Church Street. For some reason it lost its licence and was used for various purposes, one of which was Daisy Bailie's Fish & Chip Shop.

St John's church towers over Church Lane, also known as Dog Lane, perhaps because it is shaped like a dog's hind leg. It is strange that there is no gate into the churchyard opposite, but if you look at the wall it seems that a gap has been filled in.

Church Lane, Hales Owen.

The Finger Post, Hales Owen

(29)

12. The Finger Post

This view is one of the best of St John church and the town centre, showing how it crowns its sandstone hill. The picture was obviously made before any of the 1960s developments because now you would have to ignore Midland House. The work shop and house of Byng's, Building Contractors is in the bottom left corner; above it are the black and white cottages in Church Lane. The small outbuilding in front of them has since been demolished. In the centre of the picture is the Malt Shovel pub, seen more fully in the previous picture. You can also see the backs of the houses along Church Street, of which only Ivy House survives.

The Finger Post marked the junction of the A456 and A458, the Kidderminster and Stourbridge roads. The first ran left up Rumbow and Birmingham Street then via Hagley Street and Hagley Road to Kiddermister. When the bypass was built in 1960s it took most of the through traffic and the road number.

13. Birmingham Street Methodist Church

This handsome, chunky, Victorian display of "one hundred things you can do with polychrome bricks" is no longer used for worship. The members of the church joined the Congregationalists to form the United Reformed Church in Hagley Road, which they built in front of the Congregational Sunday School Rooms.

The main church building on the right has been transformed into a range of small shops with the gallery becoming a restaurant. It is well done and in keeping with the building's age and style. The school rooms to the left are now a picture gallery and the whole is called Cornbow Court.

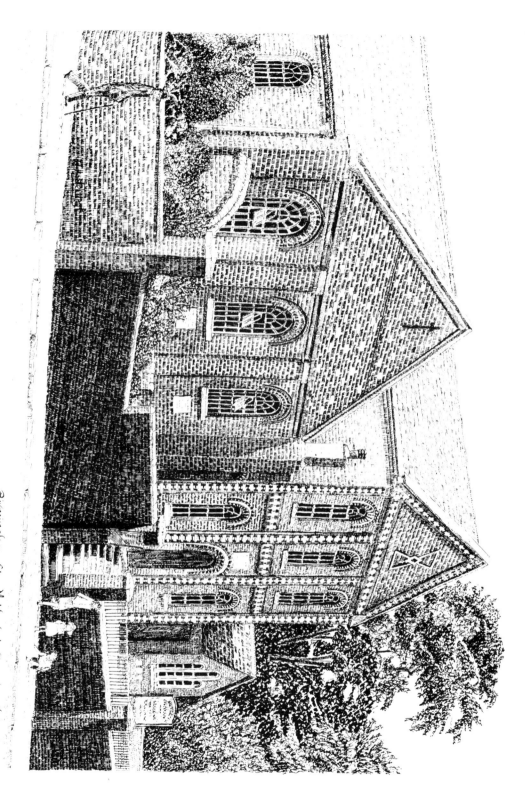

Birmingham St. Methodist Church, Hales Owen.

(32)

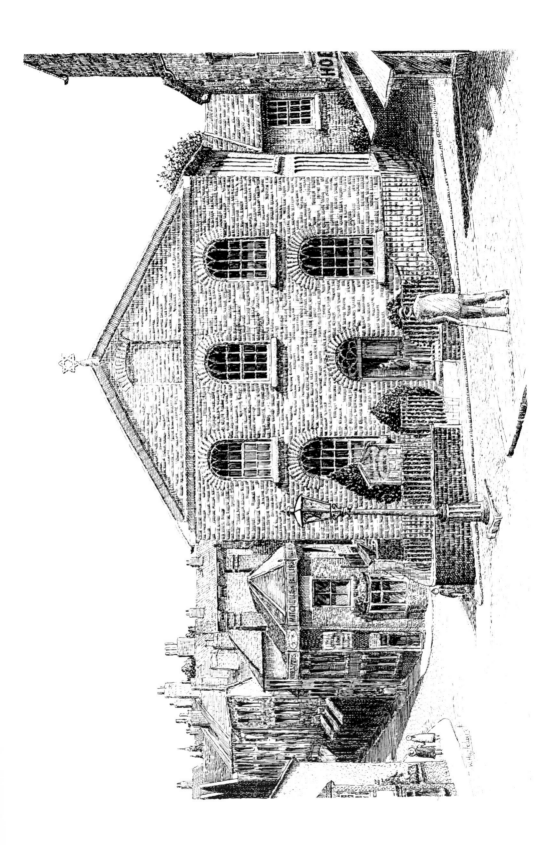

(33)

14. Congregational Church

A view from the square towards the Lyttleton Arms at the bottom of the High Street. This sedate and homely brick church formed quite a contrast with the aggressive patterning of the Methodist church in the last picture. It was built earlier in the 19th century when more broadly proportioned classical forms were nearly universal. Note the unusual stone Star of David at the roof apex, which was fixed when the gable was repaired.

This was the first chapel built in Hales Owen and appeared in the "Directory & Gazeteer of the County of Worcester 1855".

"The Independent Chapel, situate in Hagley Street, is an extensive brick building, erected by subscription in the year 1810. The interior is neatly filled with front and side Galleries and will accomodate 600 persons. There is a good Sunday School attached to the Chapel. Rev. F W Fisher, Minister."

The site is now occupied by the Midland Bank.

15. Peckingham Street

This view from Birmingham Street is similar to the cover on the first book of sketches, but shows the whole of one side of Peckingham Street in less detail.

Hollies the Butchers stood on the corner next to the gabled Globe Inn. Most people will remember it as the wine shop. Down the street were various small shops, including Len Marsh's butcher's shop. Out of view on the bottom corner would be Dancers.

The 1960s redevelopments were merciless on this type of building which had no particular architectural merits but helped form the character of towns. This is a pity, because careful removal of these mainly 18th century frontages often reveals mediaeval timber framing. The Globe was in brick which was the commonly used material. But it might also have been true of the ashlared stone butcher's building, since the firm had been established in Hales Owen for some 250 years.

Peckingham Street, Hales Owen.

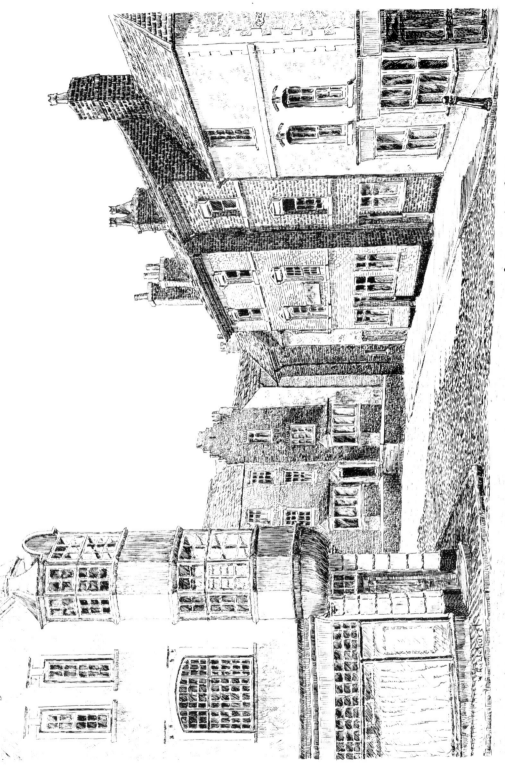

Bull Ring, Hales Owen.

(37)

16. The Bull Ring

This view down Birmingham Street looks across
the top of Peckingham Street, so Hollies the Butchers is on the right by the bollard. Next door was
the Crown Inn.

On the left was Mr Dunn's ladies hairdressers,
known as *Maison Hetty*. Bill thinks that the upper
floors with the impressive two storey oriel windows
were let out as flats.

In the centre of the picture is the Council House,
known as Cornbow House until the Council moved
there in 1930.

17. Hagley Street

The buildings have changed but not the place,
which you can recognise from the Lyttleton Arms
at the bottom corner of the High Street. Jones's shop
has gone but many local people will remember buy-
ing furniture from them.

Dancers have been established for well over a hundred years and continue to flourish as a family firm.
Now that Hollies the Butchers have gone they are
the oldest retail business in Hales Owen.

Hagley Street, Halas Owen

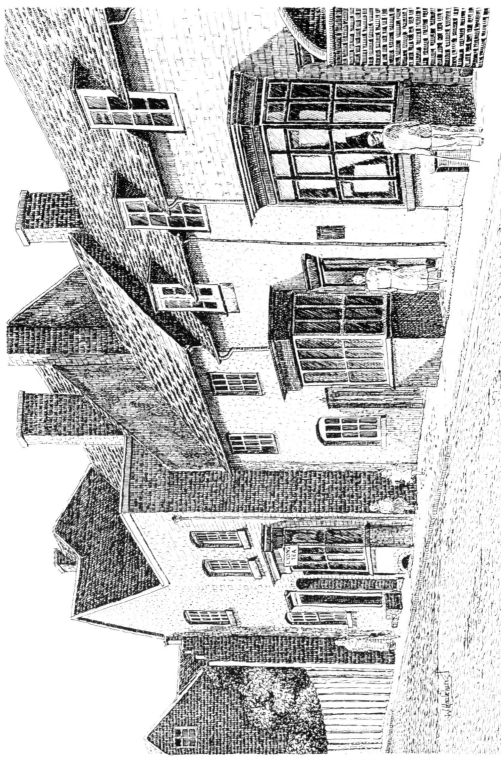

Little Cornbow Hales Owen

18. Little Cornbow

These old shops opposite the Fox pub have long since disappeared, replaced by the Job Centre and the Webb Ivory building which is now used as the Zion church.

19. Coop Bakery

The so called Model Bakery stood on its corner
site until early 1996, in its later days a battered
ruin.

Originally only the main building was erected,
but when it was rebuilt after a fire the range on
the left was added. This was used to make confect-
ionary; in the main building the upper floor housed
the flour store and mixers, while the provers and
draw ovens were on the ground floor. The building
on the right was a holding store for new bread.
Along one side were roller shutters against which
the horse vans were backed after the day's deliv-
eries for overnight loading. On the other side of
the site was a dairy which worked on for some
years after the bakery closed.

The bakery horses were stabled behind the Coop
offices in Great Cornbow, known as "The Brooklands". When the horses were unhitched after a
day's work they would amble back by themselves, down Vine Lane and over Great Cornbow.
The dairy horses were stabled in the same place
but they approached down Laurel Lane because
they had to take their carts which would not fit
through the Cornbow gate. Bill has been told
by an old bakery worker that the original stables
were in Birmingham Street behind the Mission.

Council Offices and Fire Station, Great Combow

(45)

20. Council Offices and Fire Station

Here we have another view of Great Cornbow. The brick building on the left with its jolly little Dutch gables was put up in 1846 as a police station with cells. In 1899 a new station was built in New Road and this one was taken over by the Council, who remained until they moved to Cornbow House in 1930.

The place was also used as the town's auxiliary fire station until a new one was built at Hasbury. In 1936 the local force consisted of one Chief Officer two full time drivers and nineteen volunteer firemen.

A slightly different view of Great Cornbow appeared in the first book of sketches which showed the right side and featured the jettied, timber framed building. You would also recognise the humped curb which is still there but bigger and now in front of the Swimming Pool.

The building at the bottom of the hill was Brooklands, the Coop offices.

21. Grange Mill

Even a small stream can power a watermill and the River Stour turned many. Most probably drove forging hammers but Grange Mill ground corn on the Grange Estate. It stood on the edge of the present cricket ground. The picture shows the millpond from which water was directed through a leat, or channel, onto a overshot wheel.

Undershot water wheels had the bottom segment in the stream, the breastshot type had water delivered into buckets at three quarter height, whilst overshot wheels had the leat deliver over the wheel to strike the top of the downstream side. Wispy thin memories of school physics may remind you that for some reason connected with the mechanics of levers, the overshot was the most efficient.

Local children used the millpond to fish for tiddlers and swim in spite of notices to the contrary. The mill and its pond disappeared in 1958 when the town expanded and the bypass was built.

Grange Mill, off Dogkennel Lane, Hales Owen.

Summer Hill, Hales Owen

22. Summer Hill

These old views of Summer Hill are at first rather puzzling. The picture in the first book of sketches was from the town, but this one looking down from the south is almost unrecognisable. The building of the new shopping centre and the ring road sliced through the lower part of Summer Hill.

The only portion left within the ring road with just enough space for a small, currently empty shop, and Clent Books. This sketch shows what is left of the outer portion of Summer Hill and is still a favourite view from the top at Wax-lands.

23. The Fox

This brick building still stands at the junction of
Great and Little Cornbow, but is no longer a pub.
In fact, it is hard to recognise at all, since the
door has been moved to one side and a big modern
window fitted, the front has been plastered and
white washed and it has become an office. For
that matter, you can no longer get Coopers Ales.

The Fox, great Cornbow, Hales Owen.

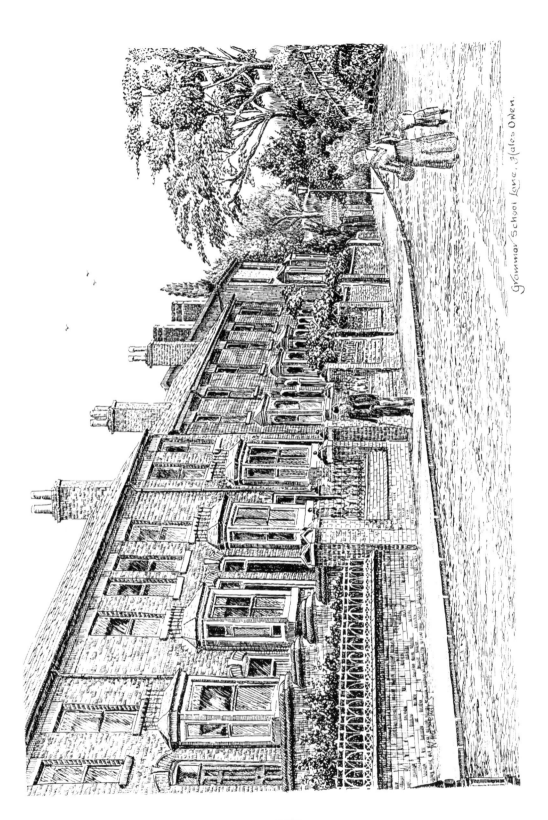

Grammar School Lane, Hales Owen.

24. Grammar School Lane

This quiet street was a cul de sac before it was connected to Old Hawne Lane. These reticent Victorian houses seem impregnable behind their high walls, railings and spiked bays. Some excellent recent renovation should make them last well into the next century.

25. Technical School

Technical education started in Hales Owen around 1900 at the school in Grammar School Lane and elsewhere. In 1939 it was rehoused in this purpose built college in Furnace Lane, at the back of the Grammar School. It has since merged with the Grammar School to form The Earls High School.

Educational buildings seem to have developed their own types of architecture. Between the wars it was usually this bland and vaguely classical approach. Here is the inevitable bellcote, the wide windows with square panes and columned door crowned with a broken pediment. Many off us remember this type of school or college as having pleasant buildings, whatever we thought of what went on inside.

Hales Owen Technical College

The Loyal Lodge. Furnace Hill, Hales Owen.

26. Loyal Lodge

As the name suggests, this pub in Furnace Hill has
its roots in Freemasonry and was originally named
"The Loyal Lodge of Freegivers". The plate over
the door shows the date 1736, but what the shield
with the initials G IM mean we have not been able
to discover. They might be the initials of the first
owner; let us know if you have any information.

27. Coombs Wood Works

The Dudley Number 2 Canal in the foreground of
the picture was opened in 1797. It ran from the
Number 1 Canal at the mouth of Dudley Tunnel
and curved round the hill to the Netherton Tunnel,
through which a branch took it to meet the Birmingham Canal at Dudley Port. The main line ran
on through Rowley Regis and Coombs Wood and
then followed the Stour Valley through Hales Owen
to cross Manor Lane near the Black Horse. Soon it
curved east into the notorious two and a half mile
Lapal Tunnel to Selly Oak and joined the Worcester
& Birmingham Canal. With transport links to Birmingham, Wolverhampton and the River Severn, and
from there to most parts of the country, Coombes
Wood was an excellent place for heavy engineering.
Bill's sketch shows something else typical of the
Black Country, a beautiful hilly green landscape
as a backdrop to industry.

Coombs Wood Works started in 1860 when Abra-
ham Barnsley bought one acre of land by the canal
from Lord Lyttleton. He started making tubes for
gas, water pipes and bedsteads. In 1862 the business was taken over by Noah Hingley & Sons,
and later by Henry Howard who amalgamated
with Lloyd & Lloyd in 1870. The manufacturing
process used gas welding from 1890, and later an
electrical process under rights secured from Russia
called the Bernados System.

Lloyd & Lloyd merged with Stewarts and Menzies,
and the new company continued to be known as
Stewarts & Lloyds long after it became part of
British Steel.

Coombs Wood Works.

Somers Row, Hales Owen.

28. Somers Row

These attractive little brick houses have long disappeared under the Forge TradingrEstate. The street was just off Forge Lane and is now called Somers Road. If you are still in doubt, the distinctive shape of Walter Somers works explains everything, including the name of the Row.

The building with the bay windows at the far end of the row was the Railway Inn, earlier known as the Bridge Tavern after a small wooden bridge over the River Stour.

Around 1740 a family called Connop lived in this area and remained for many years. Before the arrival of the railway and Somers works it was known as "Connop's Hole". Descendants of the family still live in and around Hales Owen.

29. Walter Somers Works

In 1866 a young man from Derbyshire borrowed
£100 from his father and took a lease of an ironworks
on Mucklow Hill. Here Walter Somers forged anchors
and chains from wrought iron. At first the business
struggled, but in 1870 they turned to making railway axles and buffers which improved their prospects.
Later they installed steam hammers so that heavier
forgings could be made and obtained work from the
Admiralty.

This association strengthened during the First World
War, and for the first time women were employed,
machining the forgings for 15 inch shells. Walter
Somers died in 1917 leave the works to his sons,
Seth and Frank.

Bill's wife's family worked for Somers. Her father
Horace Bagley, Uncle Bill Bagley and Uncle Arthur
Bradley spent most of their working lives there.
Bill's contribution was to install Somers's first
computer.

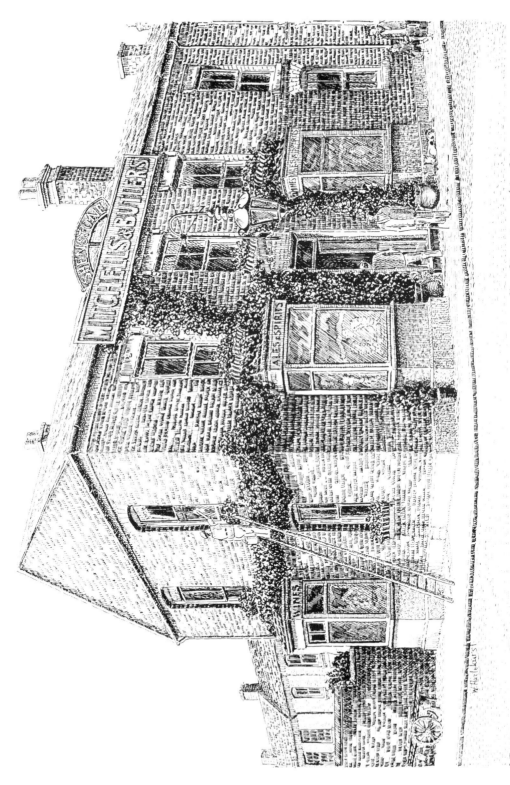

The Shenstone, Hales Owen.

W Hartshurst

(65)

30. The Shenstone

This comfortable, ivy grown pub stood where the Tarmac Building stands today, at the junction of Bromsgrove Road and Whitehall. The island at the bottom of Mucklow Hill is fairly new; there used to be traffic lights and the hill seemed much steeper. On several occasions the brakes of heavy lorries failed and they ran backwards into the Shenstone.

The name still survives as many people refer to the junction as the Shenstone Island, which is rather a distant reminder of Hales Owen's famous William Shenstone.

31. The Priory

This is no ancient ruin, but an 18th century folly
built by William Shenstone in the landscaped grounds
of The Leasowes. These rich man's extravagances are
a study in themselves and certain architects special-
ised in them. One of the best known was Sanderson
Miller who designed the mock castles and temples at
Hagley Hall, and the amazing miniature castle on
Edge Hill in south Warwickshire.

The "Priory" stood by Breaches Pool in Shenstone's
chain of water features, and the stonework is said
to have been taken from the Abbey. There was some
friendly rivalry between Shenstone and Lord Lyttleton who built Hagley Hall's mock castle at the
same time as the Priory, again using material from
the Abbey.

Old engravings show the Priory near the old Leasowes Farm and give a hint of the beautiful scene
Shenstone created on our doorstep. The Priory
lasted until it was demolished 1958.

The Priory. Hales Owen

(68)

The Black Horse, Manor Lane, Stoke Owen.

32. The Black Horse

It was not pure chance that located the Black Horse half way up Manor Lane, for just in front of this old pub the Dudley No 2 Canal crossed under the road on its way to the Lapal Tunnel. There was no towpath through it, so the boatmen had to "leg" the boat through, that is, lie on their backs and walk along the tunnel wall. They probably needed fuel for the two and a half miles of blackness between here and Selly Oak, and men who had just come through would need to recover.

The Manor Pit was opened in 1866 to get coal from the southern end of the famous Thirty Foot Seam of coal, so the Black Horse would have seen miners. Other customers would have come from the Lapal Works of which you can see the roof behind the pub.

The canal has gone, its hump back bridge blown up when Manor Lane was widened, and its place has been taken by a car park. Lapal Works has disappeared and the back and front of the pub are reversed, with a smart new entrance on the other side.

33. Hawne Farm

The gabled farmhouse in the picture stood at the
top of what is now Fairmile Road. It looks more
Victorian than 18th century, but was once part of
Hawne House. This was the birthplace in 1783 of
Thomas Attwood, who became Birmingham's first
MP and a Parliamentary reformer. The land was
in the hands of his family until 1872.

Hawne House was a rambling mansion about a mile
from Hales Owen which looked over the Stour Valley.
Until the mid 19th century this would have been a
picturesque position commanding fine views of roll-
ing countryside. However, the gradual approach of
the Industrial Revolution in the form of collieries,
iron works and forges with their thousand chimneys
made the house unliveable. The oldest part was demolished leaving only the left wing, which then became
known as Hawne Farm. At the same time an old
cherry orchard was lost. The farm also vanished in
the 1960s redevelopment.

Hawne Farm, Hales Owen

v. Hazlehurst

Lapal House

(73)

34. Lapal House

Lapal House has changed its features and looks much smaller than in a drawing by the artist David Parkes, probably done in the late 18th century. From this we can judge that it was originally of similar proportions to The Leasowes (Sketch 1). Bill's view of Lapal House is recent. It lies hidden down secretive Lapal Lane which plays the wonderful trick of seeming to be miles from town.

From 1753 to 93 this was the home of John Scott Hylton who had been born in Warley in 1725. He was a friend of William Shenston and and deeply interested in the arts. At Lapal House he organised musical evenings and had many famous visitors. T Mayer RA came to paint Mr Horne who owned The Leasowes, and the painter Sir Joshua Reynolds made a portrait of Lady Jane Halliday, a later resident.

Mr Hylton died in 1803, and it is said that a large blue stone was set into the floor at the west end of St John's church bearing the inscription:

> "In memory of John Scott Hylton, Esq. late of Lapal House near Hales owen, who died 23rd, february, 1793, aged 67 years. A Safe comp-anion and easy friend."

Little else is recorded about the history of Lapal House. It is now a well maintained and well run retirement home which is still set in countryside with landscaped gardens for the residents to enjoy. Mr Tony Billingham, the present owner, keeps up John Hylton's musical tradition and runs a jazz band. Bill would like to thank him for allowing us to reproduce this sketch.

35. Carter's Lane Baptist Church

The Baptists in this area originally held their services and sunday school in cottages at Illey. Their first church was built on this land which had been leased by Joseph Perry. Lord Lyttleton was the owner and in time gave the church the freehold, together with further land to build schoolrooms. The early chapel seated one hundred people and opened on Easter Monday 1811.

In the late 1930s the old building was demolished when Carter's Lane was widened as part of a housing development. The brick church in the picture was built with the compensation in 1939, and continues to flourish.

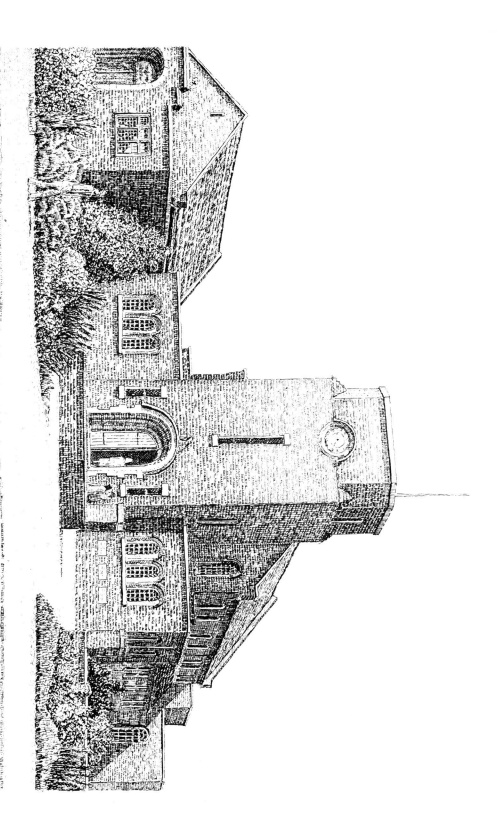

Carters Lane Baptist Church, Halesowen

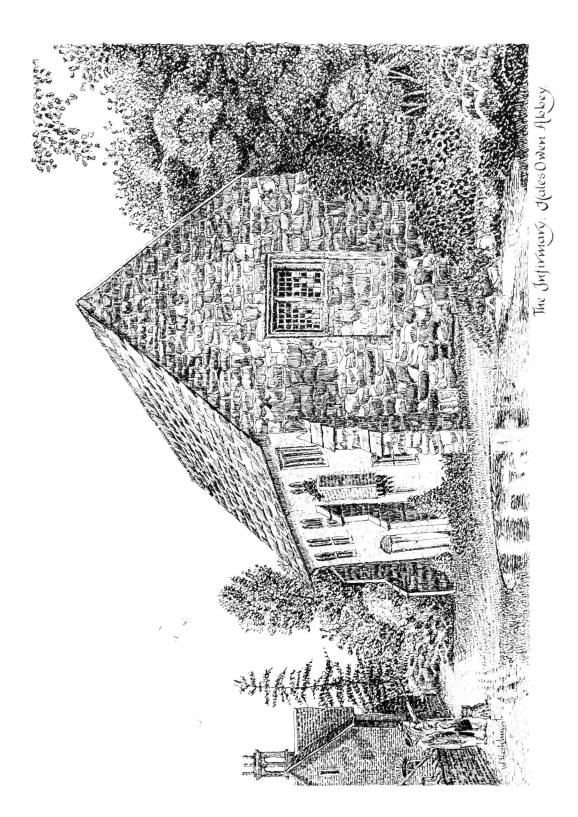

The Infirmary, Hales Owen Abbey.

36. The Abbey Infirmary

The windows show that this ancient building once had two storeys; some people think it was the Abbots dwelling. The wooden roof is still supported by the original king post trusses, but most parts of the structure have been repaired at some stage of its long life since the twelfth century.

When the religious houses were suppressed by Henry VIII at the Reformation, the Abbey land became a farm and for many years this building was used as a barn and machinery store. It was restored in 1989 and the site is now open to the public on weekends through the summer. Go and see it while you can.

37. The Cottage Hospital

This rather domestic looking building with the
Town Hall sized porch was called The Mount
and stood directly behind Tenterfield School.
It was Hales Owen's cottage hospital, taking
accident and sickness cases in twenty beds
supported by voluntary contributions. Note the
swan on the pediment. How did that get there?

Within the town there were two other hospitals.
Hayley Green was first an isolation hospital for
ordinary infectious diseases. Later it became a
geriatric hospital until closure in 1996. The
other hospital was at Grove Lane, Hasbury which
handled smallpox. It no longer exists but stood
between Brackenfield Road and Fernbank Close.

The Mount closed as a hospital and was bought
by a farrier, then sold again for conversion
into flats. It was demolished quite some years
ago.

The Mount Cottage Hospital, Bishopstoke

Hare & Hounds, Hasbury, Hales Owen

(81)

38. The Hare & Hounds

The modern Hare & Hounds stands near the top of the hill on Hagley Road, Hasbury. This earlier version occupied the car park of the present building. You can play "guess the date" of the picture by studying the car, which we reckon is a Ford, and speculate about the date of the present pub.

39. New Street

New Street has entirely disappeared. If streets left ghosts, this one would waft about in the high flats between Hagley Road and Highfield Lane, for it was an extension of Red Leasowes from Cross Street.

In this view which looks down into the town, the shop on the right was Williams's which sold hardware and paraffin. Britton's owned the shop on the left by the local pub, the British Arms.

New Street, Hales Owen.

W. Hadchins

(84)

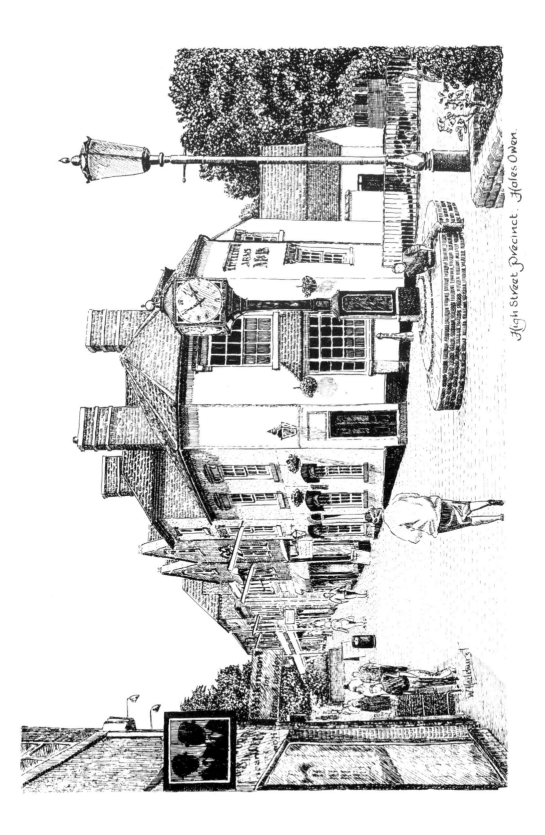

High Street Precinct. Hales Owen.

40. High Street Precinct

This sketch shows the older part of the High Street with its modern embellishments of block paving, flower beds and the clock. To the left are the flat roofed and featureless modern shops. Why could we not have kept the old buildings on this side as well, and put the shopping centre to the rear of them. We might then have had a town centre of real charm. It is not a question of architectural distinction, just of harmony and good manners.

Time is not like that clock and cannot be put back, but planners and the public are now much wiser and more knowledgeable about development issues, giving hope for better handling of future schemes. Hales Owen had its revolution too soon.

We hope you have enjoyed this second pen and ink expedition through the past and present streets of Hales Owen. Bill is working on a book of sketches around Stratford upon Avon but welcomes suggest ions of buildings and scenes in most parts of the Midlands. Call at his shop and pass on your ideas and memories.

MEMORY CORNER

THE PICTURE FRAMING GALLERY
HAGLEY ROAD,
(opp. Quarry Lane)
HASBURY, HALES OWEN
TEL: 021-585 0506

... publishing interesting books ...

Quercus is a regional publisher specialising in books about the West Midlands, Warwickshire, Worcestershire, Shropshire and south Staffs, with some some books on Wales.

We are interested in the region yesterday, today and tomorrow; in landscapes and trees, meadows and flowers, history, battles, lords and kings, castles and churches, bridges and tunnels. We want to know about industries and towns, people and customs, playgrounds and parks, myths and hauntings. We are interested in anything you find interesting.

Currently in print are *Midland Castles (£7.50), The Trackway of the Cross (£3.50), Sketches of Halesowen (£7.50), Midland Woods & Forests (£7.95), Midlands Ghosts & Hauntings (£6.95) Sketches of Birmingham (£7.50), Midland Rivers (£7.95), Sketches of Bromsgrove (£7.50), Heart in my Boots (£3.95)* and *Australian Williams (£3.50).*

Midland Woods & Forests was the first book in a series on the geography and natural history of the Midlands. *Midland Rivers* was the second, to be followed by *Midland Lakes & Ponds.*

Midlands Parks, Midland Murders & Mysteries, Historic Houses & Gardens in Staffs, Shropshire and West Midlands, Coaching Days in the Midlands, and *Midland Spirits & Spectres* are all in hand.

**8 Hillside Close, Bartley Green, Birmingham
B32 4LT   0121 550 3158
(phone or write for further details)**

WALKWAYS

DaywalkS Footpath Networks

Networks of linked paths cover each area.

Cannock Chase (£4.95)
Vale of Llangollen (£4.95)
Wyre Forest (£4.95)

Strolls & Walks

From twenty places there is a short stroll and a walk.

Strolls & Walks from Picnic Places (Midlands) (£4.95)
Strolls & Walks from Cotswold Villages (£5.50)
Strolls & Walks from Midland Villages (1996)

Long Distance Routes

Step by step guides in both directions

Centenary Way (£6.45) Heart of England Way (£6.45)
The Midland Link (1997) Birmingham to Aberystwyth (1997)
Llangollen to Snowdon (1998) Birmingham to Bala (some time)

Walks around …

Walks in specific areas by Ramblers Association groups.

Twenty Walks around Rugby (£4.75)
Walks around Coventry (£3.25)
Twenty Walks around Stourbridge (1996)

**8 Hillside Close, Bartley Green, Birmingham
B32 4LT 0121 550 3158**